# Philosophy for children

## From child to children

## Once upon a time!

# Mother owl!

## Coloring story!

# By: Bernardo Octaviano Pereira

# This book belongs to:

_______________

*I dedicate this work, firstly, to my parents who I love so much, to my teachers, to my dear aunts and to all my friends, may God bless you all infinitely!*

**Bernardo Octaviano Pereira**

05/04/2024

Once upon a time, in an enchanted forest, not far from here, full of little animals of all kinds, one day Mrs. Owl had an unusual encounter with Mr. Wolf.

talk comes and goes, that's when Mr. Wolf said he was hungry and would eat anything, and Mrs. Owl started talking;

- *Please Mr. Wolf, not like my little children, Mr. Wolf* immediately asked;

- What are
your little
owl children
like?
And the owl
lady started
talking;

*- It's easy to recognize Mr. Wolf, they are the cutest little puppies in the forest; Given the request and the charming description, he surprisingly and understandingly assured.*

-It's okay, Mrs. Owl, you can let me, I promise that I won't do any harm to your little children;

**And they went away, each one in their own direction, in a forest full of magic, some time later Mr. Wolf came across a nest full of puppies,**

*which to his eyes were strangely different, uglier than he had ever seen, naked, big-headed, noisy;*

**Without recognizing that they were Mrs. Owl's babies, Mr. Hungry Wolf, he had no doubts, he immediately began eating all of Mrs. Owl's babies that were in the nest,**

What Mr. Wolf didn't know was that, for Mrs. Owl, those puppies were the cutest in the forest, but for Mr. Wolf they weren't;

*This story teaches us that, for mothers, their children will always be the cutest, most special ones. Before judging, it is important to consider a mother's loving gaze on her puppies.*

Sometimes what may seem strange to others can seem extraordinarily beautiful in the eyes of a mother.

# The end!

www.ingramcontent.com/pod-product-compliance
Lightning Source LLC
Chambersburg PA
CBHW081958260726
48659CB00009BA/3054